Nora the Naturalist's Animals

Garden Animals

A+
Smart Apple Media

Published by Smart Apple Media, an imprint of Black Rabbit Books
P.O. Box 3263, Mankato, Minnesota 56002
www.blackrabbitbooks.com

Produced by David West 🏃 Children's Books
7 Princeton Court, 55 Felsham Road, London SW15 1AZ

Designed and illustrated by David West

Copyright © 2013 David West Children's Books

Library of Congress Cataloging-in-Publication Data

West, David, 1956-
   Garden animals / David West.
      p. cm. – (Nora the Naturalist's animals)
   Summary: "Nora the Naturalist discovers the world of Garden Animals, describing various animals and
how they live."– Provided by publisher.
   Includes index.
   ISBN 978-1-62588-003-1 (library binding)
   ISBN 978-1-62588-050-5 (paperback)
1. Garden animals–Juvenile literature. I. Title.
   QL119.W47 2014
   591.75'54–dc23
                                                                                    2013007137

Printed in China
CPSIA compliance information: DWCB13CP
010313

9 8 7 6 5 4 3 2 1

Nora the Naturalist says:
I will tell you something
more about the animal.

 Learn what this animal eats.

 Where in the world is the animal found?

 Its size is revealed!

 What animal group is it – mammal, bird, reptile, amphibian, insect, or something else?

 Interesting facts.

Contents

Insects

Gardens around the world are home to insects of all types. Over half of all animals are insects. Some are so small you need to look very closely. Others are as big as your hand.

Honey bee

Ant

Nora the Naturalist says:
Insects usually have three body segments, and six jointed legs.

Ladybug

Admiral butterfly

Some insects eat plants and some, like the ladybug, eat animals, such as other insects.

Insects are found all over the world, except in Antarctica.

All insects are arthropods. They have exoskeletons, segmented bodies, and jointed legs.

The largest insect is the **larva** of the goliath beetle which weighs 4.1 ounces (115 g) and is 4.5 inches (11.5 cm) long.

Some insects spend most of their lives as larvae. Butterfly larvae may turn into butterflies after several months as a caterpillar.

Orb-web spider

Spiders

Spiders are an important animal in the garden. The most common types weave orb webs which catch flies in their sticky threads. Spiders differ from insects as they have eight legs, and their body has just two segments.

Apart from one species, all spiders eat insects and occasionally other spiders too.

Spiders are found worldwide on every continent, except in Antarctica.

The smallest spiders are less than 0.015 inches (0.37 mm) in body length. The largest and heaviest have body lengths up to 3.5 inches (90 mm) and leg spans up to 10 inches (250 mm) wide.

Spiders are members of the arachnid family. All arachnids have eight legs.

Spiders live in nearly every habitat with the exception of the sea. There are even spiders that live underwater in ponds. These are called diving bell spiders.

Snail

Soft Bodies

Rain brings out the soft-bodied animals from their hiding places. Slugs and snails are considered pests but earthworms are good for the soil and are the gardener's friend.

The giant African land snail grows up to 15 inches (38 cm) long.

 Snails and slugs are found all over the world, except in Anarctica. They are even found in the sea.

 Snails, slugs, and earthworms all eat plants.

 Both slugs and snails are mollusks. Earthworms are members of the **annelid** family.

 Earthworms spend most of their life under the ground. They come to the surface at night, which is why they are sometimes referred to as "nightcrawlers."

Slug

Earthworm

Nora the Naturalist says:
Snails and slugs live in moist environments and must retreat to damp hiding places when the weather is dry.

9

Snakes eat small animals including lizards, other snakes, small mammals, birds, eggs, fish, snails, and insects.

Snakes are found on every continent except Antarctica. Exceptions include some large islands, such as Ireland and New Zealand, and many small islands of the Atlantic and central Pacific.

Most snakes are fairly small, around 3 feet (1 m) in length.

Snakes are members of the **reptile** family.

Snakes smell by using their forked tongues to collect particles in the air.

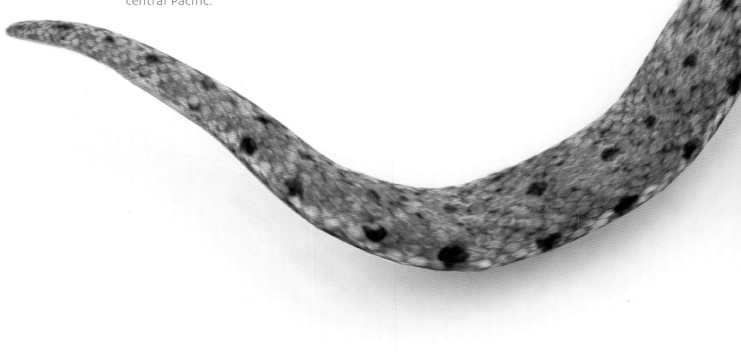

Nora the Naturalist says:
The grass snake lives in Europe and Asia. It is not poisonous and is often found near water. It feeds almost exclusively on **amphibians**.

10

Grass snake

Snakes

Depending on where you live in the world, these garden visitors can be rare or never seen at all. Some snakes are poisonous and use **venom** to kill their prey before they swallow it whole.

Tortoises

Sometimes called land turtles, these are one of the slowest moving reptiles. They occasionally make their way into gardens where there are juicy plants to feed on.

Most tortoises feed on grasses, weeds, and leafy greens.

Tortoises live on all continents except Antarctica, and on a few islands.

Tortoises vary in size from six inches (15 cm) to 5.9 feet (1.8 m) in length.

Tortoises are members of the reptile family.

Tortoise

Nora the Naturalist says:
Tortoises have big, heavy shells that are shaped like domes. They can hide inside their shells for protection against hungry predators.

Some tortoises can live to over 150 years old!

Depending on the species, songbirds eat anything from insects and worms to grain and seeds.

Songbirds vary from continent to continent. They cannot be found in Antarctica.

Songbirds are members of the perching bird family, called passerine.

Most songbirds are small, between just 5–7 inches (13–18 cm) in length.

Some songbirds, like parrots and mockingbirds, can mimic human speech.

Cardinal

Parsons finch

Grosbeak

Nora the Naturalist says:
Songbirds sing to tell other birds where they are, and also to attract a mate.

14

Songbirds

You may be lucky enough to have these beautiful animals nesting in or visiting your garden. Songbirds were given this name because they talk in songs.

Robin

Scarlet finch

Wren

House sparrow

These birds have a varied diet and eat insects, snails, baby birds, small mammals, berries, fruits, seeds, and dead animals.

Members of the crow family live on every continent except Antarctica.

The largest crows are ravens, which grow to 26 inches (65 cm).

The crow family of birds belongs to the songbird family.

Young crows and magpies play games such as "follow the leader" and "king of the mountain."

Magpie

Visiting Birds

Members of the crow family often visit gardens. They are the largest of the songbirds, and they include jays, magpies, jackdaws, ravens, and rooks.

Crow

Nora the Naturalist says: These birds are very intelligent. They recognize themselves in mirrors and use tools to get food.

Squirrels

Squirrels are tree-dwelling animals. They can often be seen running around gardens, collecting nuts. In the autumn they bury the nuts so that they can eat them during winter.

Nora the Naturalist says:
Squirrels live in a nest called a drey. When food is scarce during the winter months they rely on their buried food.

They are mainly plant eaters, living on nuts, seeds, conifer cones, fruits, fungi, and green vegetation, but many will eat insects, lizards, and birds' eggs.

Squirrels have always lived in the Americas, Europe, Asia, and Africa, and have been introduced to Australia.

Squirrels vary in size from the African pygmy squirrel at 2.8–3.9 inches (7–10 cm) in length to the gray squirrel which is 22 inches (55 cm) long including its tail.

Squirrels are members of the rodent family, which are mammals.

As well as gray squirrels there are black and red squirrels.

Gray squirrel

19

Rabbits

If you live in the countryside your garden may get visited by these small, white-tailed mammals. Gardeners don't like them as they eat garden crops such as lettuces and carrots.

Rabbits feed by grazing on grass, some flowering plants, and leafy weeds.

Rabbits live on every continent except Antarctica. Half the world's rabbit population lives in North America.

Their size can range from 8 inches (20 cm) to 20 inches (50 cm) in length.

Rabbits are members of the mammal family, and are closely related to hares.

The European rabbit lives in underground burrows, or rabbit holes. A group of burrows is called a warren.

Nora the Naturalist says:
A male rabbit is called a buck, and a female is a doe. A young rabbit is a kitten or kit.

Rabbits

Foxes

The red fox is a recent visitor to towns and cities. Many of these beautiful mammals have moved from the countryside to find food in the gardens and streets of our populated areas.

Nora the Naturalist says:
The urban fox has become a problem for some people by disrupting garbage cans, stealing chickens, and wrecking gardens.

Red foxes

Foxes eat small mammals, reptiles, amphibians, scorpions, grasses, berries, fruit, fish, birds, eggs, insects, and food from garbage cans.

Foxes live in all types of habitats, from the Arctic to deserts. They can be found on all continents except Antarctica.

Foxes are members of the mammal family.

The red fox is the largest of the true foxes. They are 18–35 inches (45–90 cm) in body length with tails measuring 13–21 inches (32–53 cm).

The tail of a red fox is called a brush.

Glossary

annelid
The family of segmented worms species including ragworms, earthworms and leeches.

amphibians
Animals capable of living on land and in water.

larva
An early stage of many insects before they change into adults.

reptile
A cold-blooded, usually egg-laying animal, such as a snake, lizard, crocodile, and turtle.

venom
Poison.

Index